HUMAN RIGHTS AND THE LGBTQI+ COMMUNITY

VOLUME 2, ISSUE 4 OF BRILLOPEDIA

RISHA P K

Contents

Preface

"Start writing, no matter what. The water does not flow until the faucet is turned on".

• Louis L'Amour

Hundreds of students and professors are contributing their work to Brillopedia, we are here to provide ample information about Law and Contemporary issues. Our aim is to provide a platform for today's generation to express their views and ideas on law and contemporary law.

Publication

This research paper is published in volume 2, issue 4 of Brillopedia

Author

Risha P K is a fifth year law student from RV institute of Legal Studies

CHAPTER ONE

Abstract

The rights concerned about LGBTQ+ are not a neoteric issue, the rights of the humans belonging to this community were always there in question. The questions of their rights are always lingering in society. The term LBGTQI+ is an umbrella term for people who have different sexuality and gender identity. LGBTQI+ community includes people who are Gay, Lesbian, Trans, Queer, Intersex, etc. the Indian legal system has only acknowledged their community recently through decriminalization of part of section 377 of the IPC which had a provision that criminalized same-gender sexual activities. It used to be seen as unnatural and as a crime before the aforesaid judgment in the case *Navtej Singh Johar v. Union of India*. Like every other human being people from that community also deserves to live with dignity and freedom. Someone's preference of whom they choose to love or what they choose to become or who they are shall not be a barrier or a reason to infringe on their fundamental rights. Human beings irrespective of their sexual preference, caste, creed, origin, etc deserved to be treated as human beings.

CHAPTER TWO

Introduction

The lesbian, gay, transgender, queer, intersex, etc; communities are considered to be a minority whose rights are being violated all over the world. Hilary Clinton in one of the U.N. conferences mentioned this community of people to be the "invisible minority" as violations of their rights are not seen due to the cultural and customs barrier of that particular country. Their rights are being violated as people from this community are exposed to bullying, being kicked out of their homes, not being able to complete their education, not getting support from families, not getting jobs to do and ending up in the streets, some begging, some forced into prostitution, etc. Their rights to residence, the right to education, the right to do a job, etc are denied. Due to these issues people from this community are scared to 'come out' to express their true identity, which again is a violation of their right to express themselves. Many LBGTQI+ people do not come out in fear of these situations and end up compromising their lives and marrying and having kids and starting a family, without not being able to express what they want. The social stigma and discrimination against the LBGTQI+ people shall change for them to be able live freely as any other citizen of this country.

As per research the chance of mental health issues like depression and anxiety are more likely in this group of people because of their bitter life experience due to social stigma and lack of support from their family, peers, and government. Suicide rates are also high in this community people than in the general population due to the harassment and discrimination and lack of mental health support available. In India, some media even used derogatory terms for reporting the suicides of transgender and intersex people. Many queer people around the world are forced to take anti-conversion therapy when it's not practically possible to psychologically change someone's sexual preference, or gender identity as they are the result of genetic variations in the human body, many other people of this community are subjected to molestation, forced marriages, torture killing, domestic violence, illegal arrest, medical abuse, etc.

Like every other citizen of a country people belonging to this community too have the right to live and die with dignity, but like any other 'minority' in a country, this community is also denied their respect, dignity, freedom, and dreams. Let's remind ourselves that "gay rights are human rights" and dive deep into the human rights violations of the LGBTQI+ community.

CHAPTER THREE

Human rights and the LGBTQI+ community

Discrimination and harassment against the LGBTQI+ community are against the principle laid in the Universal Declaration of Human Rights. Many cultures and customs around the world are immersed in homophobia and transphobia. The people of this community face discrimination in all fields of society such as education, the medical system, etc; many countries are obligated to protect human rights without any discrimination yet still many countries are still imposing punishments for same-sex relationships and same-sex sexual activities, some countries consider these illegal and against the nature.

The discrimination differs with their socio-eco-political situations and conditions. For example, the discrimination and harassment of a gay person belonging to the upper class will not be the same as what a gay person from a marginalized group be facing. It will be different but all humans deserved to be treated humanely and with dignity irrespective of what they are or are not.

"So long as people face criminalization, bias, and violence based on their sexual orientation, gender identity, and sex characteristics, we must redouble our efforts to end these violations," Antonio Guterres, UN Secretary-General, on 25 September 2018. The united nations have established treaties in concern with this discrimination since the 1990s with the complied countries.

Many countries are accepting the LGBTQI+ community and can see past their sexual preferences or gender identity; as result, many people from this community are holding government offices, becoming actively part of a government system, and leading a nation.

To come past this discrimination against this community there is no necessity for a new set of rules or statutory acts, treating them equally as any other citizen is the simple solution. International human rights have established laws in the UDHR, etc; which point out a state's duty to provide equal rights to the LGBTQI people.

Which are as follows:-

- The state shall protect against transphobic and homophobic hate crimes.
- It shall decriminalize laws against same-sex relationships or different gender identities.
- It shall prevent cruel or inhuman or degrading treatment against LGBTQI+ people.
- It shall make laws to prohibit discrimination against LGBTQI+ people.
- It shall provide a platform or space to express themselves (LGBTQI+ people) and to assemble peacefully.

[1]In modern times many countries have took the effort to bring up new laws and rules to protect and up bring this community such as decriminalizing same-sex relationships, providing awareness to frontline workers, anti-bullying schemes in schools, penalizing hate crimes against LGBTQI+ people, ensuring that asylum laws recognize sexual orientation and gender identity as a basis for claiming persecution and enabling LGBT persons fleeing persecution to avoid returning to countries or territories where their freedom is threatened.

The UN has been collaborating with Member States to oppose criminalizing and discriminating against people because of their sexual orientation or gender identity. While there is still widespread discrimination against LGBTQI+ people in the globe today, over 30 nations have decriminalized homosexuality in the previous 20 years. Despite opposition, the U.N., affiliated NGOs, and officials of Member States have been working assiduously to uphold the human rights of LGBT people. Undoubtedly, the U.N. is moving closer to the inclusion of LGBT rights in our fundamental human rights today under the direction of then Secretary-General Ban Ki-moon.

[1]Are LGBT rights human rights? Recent developments at the United Nations, India, *available at:* https://www.apa.org/international/pi/2012/06/un-matters. (last visited on november 27, 2022)

CHAPTER FOUR

Navtej Singh Johar v. Union of India

This case laid out the landmark judgment decriminalizing same-sex sex stating that consensual same sex is not an unnatural act. In reading Section 377, the four judges (DipakMisra, R. F. Nariman, D. Y. Chandrachud, and InduMalhotra) uniformly identified infringement of basic rights. They discovered that Section 377 violates Articles 14 and 15 of the Constitution by discriminating against people based on their sexual orientation and/or gender identity. Additionally, they determined that Section 377 contravenes Article 21's guarantees of the right to life, dignity, and personal autonomy. Finally, they discovered that it violates Article 19(1) (a) right to freedom of speech, which prevents LGBT people from completely realizing who they are.

CHAPTER FIVE

Conclusion

The discrimination faced by LGBTQI+ people is not something new. They have been oppressed and discriminated against from the time they started to express themselves. To change this situation of divergence the Government as the representative of the state shall bring in new schemes and laws to protect this community, and follow the treaties that had been established by the U.N. The change shall start from the grass root level kids shall be taught about different sexualities and gender identities in schools, and awareness programs shall be established in every category or level of society. This community and its people shall be normalized through representations in the cinemas, by holding government offices, winning gold medals, to put it in simple words, they shall be normalized by just 'letting them be' and by not treating them differently. One thing, we as a society, shall keep in our mind is that "gay rights are human rights"

"To those who are lesbian, gay, bisexual, or transgender, let me say: You are not alone. Your struggle for an end to violence and discrimination is a shared struggle. Any attack on you is an attack on the universal values of the United Nations I have sworn to defend and uphold. Today, I stand with you, and I call upon all countries and people to stand with you, too".

-Ban Ki-Moon, Former Secretary-General of the United Nations.[1]

[1]Are LGBT rights human rights? Recent developments at the United Nations, India, *available at:* https://www.apa.org/international/pi/2012/06/un-matters. (last visited on november 27, 2022)